I Joh...

als. Dunk... Prun...

1 John 5:14-15.
Dr. Barnhart

The Prayer Manual

Warring in the Heavenlies

By

Dr. Brenda D. Howard

Copyright © 2013 by Brenda D. Howard

ISBN 978-0-7414-9691-1

Printed in the United States of America

Published September 2013

INFINITY PUBLISHING
1094 New DeHaven Street, Suite 100
West Conshohocken, PA 19428-2713
Toll-free (877) BUY BOOK
Local Phone (610) 941-9999
Fax (610) 941-9959
Info@buybooksontheweb.com
www.buybooksontheweb.com

Table of Contents

Purpose of the Prayer Manual

The purpose of this prayer manual is to introduce you to prayer and its components.

The Bible tells us to "Pray without ceasing..." (I Thessalonians 5:17). Sometimes new converts don't know how to pray. This manual is to help them have some guidelines to make praying easier.

We understand that praying is talking to God, who loves us and is concerned about us. In Prayer we talk to God and listen for His response. Talking to God is just like talking to someone you are familiar with, someone whom you have a relationship with. As you pray, you build a close relationship to the one you are praying to.

Sometimes having a mental formula will help us to pray more effectively. By all means, I am not suggesting that acronyms are necessary to talk to God but may be helpful. Some of the acronyms are P-r-a-y-e-r and A-c-t-s. The meaning will be explained in the manual.

The manual begins with the Brazen Altar, which was in the Old Testament tabernacle. This was the altar in the outer court where the sacrifices were made. The Brazen Altar leads to the Golden Altar of incense where the prayers were offered up with incense as a sweet smelling savor to God. This was just a shadow of what was to come (Hebrews 10:1-4). But when you understand the Old Testament prototype then you will understand the importance of Jesus Christ's suffering and dying on the cross. He (Jesus Christ) was the perfect sacrifice. Everything needed to reconcile man back unto God the Father was in Jesus. It was satisfied in the death, burial and resurrection of Jesus Christ. It was important that the middle wall of partition be torn down (Matthew 27:51) and Jesus Christ occupies the "Mercy Seat" so that the people of God can pray to our Father in heaven without needing another High Priest. The earthly High Priest went in to the "Holy of Holies" once a year to offer up sacrifices for the sins of the people (Hebrews 10:3;9:1-7). Jesus Christ became that High Priest that went in once and for all and through His blood made a way for us to approach a true and living God (Hebrews 9:12;10:10). Through His (Jesus) blood, we have access to our Father (God).

This brings us to the New Covenant when the middle wall of partition was torn from top to bottom and now as born again children of God we can pray to our God in secret who will reward us openly (Matthew 6:6).

This manual is designed to give a basic and simple means of bringing you into the presence of God. Prayer should be fervent (James5:16) and through the Holy Spirit.

Section 1

The Brazen Altar

Exodus 27:1-8

The "Brazen Altar" represented the place of sacrifice, which was figurative of the sacrifice, which was made on the Cross of Calvary. This altar was the first piece of furniture one saw when they entered the tabernacle; all of the other services were linked to the brazen altar.

This altar was the place of suffering. The animals sacrificed here were symbolic of the substitutionary sacrifice needed for salvation. Hebrews 9:22 said, "And according to the law *almost all things are purified with blood, and without the shedding of blood there is no remission for sin."*

The offering placed on the altar was completely consumed by the fire, which continually burned upon the altar. The fire lifted up what was on the altar. As the offering was consumed by fire, the smoke of sacrifice ascended up to God. As the brazen altar lifted up its offering, so the cross of Christ lifted him up as an offering for sin before God. Jesus said, "And I, if I be lifted up from the earth, I will draw all men unto me" (John 12:32). Fire represents the judicial nature of God. The brazen altar depicts the judgment that must be offered for sin. The fire on the altar was never to go out; it was always burning day and night. By the continual fire on the altar the Israelites learned that God was always ready to receive them through sacrifice. "And the Spirit and the bride say, "come!" And let him who hears say, "Come!" And let him who thirsts come... (Revelation 22:17). Salvation is available to all that will surrender to the Lord Jesus Christ.

The construction of the brazen altar was divinely given and each measurement and the materials used to make the altar had a symbolic meaning. In Exodus 27:1; the brazen altar was made of "shittim or acacia wood. Acacia or shittim wood was beautiful, light and basically indestructible. The genus, "acacia seyal," was the wood used in the Old Testament to make the "Ark of the Covenant." The "acacia" was symbolic of the humanity of Jesus Christ. Acacia wood is the only wood that could grow in the desert. It was covered with bronze or brass, which represented the judgment for sin. Jesus became the perfect sacrifice for sin, after His sacrifice on the cross there is no more need for the brazen altar. The altar was built with many parts:

a.) Grates – The word grate comes from the root word which means "to plait" or "twist." The grate held the sacrifice and wood for the fire that consumed it. The grate was the same height as the mercy seat. The sacrifice of Christ for sin is on the same level as the throne of God. By His sacrifice on the cross Jesus did everything which righteousness required for man to be accepted by God.

b.) Staves – The brazen altar was designed to go with the people of God anywhere they went. Two staves or poles were provided for this purpose. The handles symbolized that there are two ways that the Gospel is carried into the entire world by both the death and resurrection of Jesus Christ. Both parts of the gospel must be equally emphasized, the death and resurrection unless it becomes unequally balanced. The two staves speak of the work of Christ proclaimed in the Old and New Testament.

c.) Rings – The rings, as unending circles, speak of the eternal. They were overlaid with bronze or brass, which speaks of eternal judgment from eternity. The rings for the altar were four, which is the number of the world. The judgment, which Christ bore in His own body because of man's sin was for the entire world.

There were five (5) utensils and five (5) animals used at the brazen altar. Grace is "unmerited favor;" favor that we don't deserve. In numerology the number five (5) represents GRACE. At the brazen altar the animals became the substitutionary sacrifice. It was not eternal it had to be repeated each year to satisfy the penalty for sin.

The utensils used at the brazen altar were:

a.) Pan – This was used to hold the ashes

b.) Shovels – Used for picking up the ashes

c.) Basin – Used to hold the blood sacrifice

d.) Flesh-hooks – Used to arrange the sacrifice on the grate of the altar

e.) Fire-pan or censer– Used to carry the fire to the altar

There were five animals used as sacrifices:

a.) Lamb (without blemish, of the first year)

b.) Bullock

c.) Goat

d.) Heifer

e.) Turtledove

As you see the sacrifice on the brazen altar was the first step to the golden altar of incense, which was the place of prayer. You must be saved in order for God to hear your prayers.

John 9:31 Now we know that; God heareth not sinners: but if any man be a worshipper of God, and doeth his will, him he heareth.

Those that have been washed in the blood of Jesus have the right to approach the "throne of grace."

II Chronicles 7:14 God says; If my people, which are called by my name, shall humble themselves, and pray, and seek my face, and turn from their wicked ways; then will I hear from heaven, and will forgive their sin, and will heal their land.

Sacrifice on the "Brazen Altar" led to the "Golden Altar of Incense."

Section 1 Memory Quiz

Scripture to Remember

II Chronicles 7:14 If My people, which are called by My name, shall humble themselves, and pray, and seek My face, and turn from their wicked ways; then will I hear from heaven and will forgive their sins, ands will heal their land.

Memory Questions

1. The offering placed on the _____ was completely _____ by the fire which continually _____ upon the altar.

2. _____ or _____ wood was beautiful, light and basically indestructible.

3. The _____ lamb was without _____, of the first year.

4. The _____ _____ was symbolic of the humanity of Jesus Christ.

5. _____ is unmerited favor.

Section 1 Prayer Journal

During and after prayer it is good to write down the thoughts that: come to your mind, people that rise up in your spirit or anything that God will reveal. Learn to write down what God is saying so that you can go back and meditate on what He has revealed to you.

Section 2

The Golden Altar of Incense

The "Golden Altar of Incense" sat in front of the curtain that separated the Holy Place from the Holy of Holies. This altar was smaller than the brazen altar but taller than any article in the tabernacle symbolizing the exalted nature of God.

The way to the "Golden Altar" is through the sacrifice made at the "brazen altar." The way to God under the New Covenant is through His Son Jesus Christ. Jesus was the perfect sacrifice, the Lamb that was without blemish of the first year. John saw Jesus on the Isle of Patmos as, a Lamb that had been slain from the very foundation of the world. Sacrifice (brazen altar) precedes prayer (Golden Altar). Prayer is based on what was done on Calvary.

The Golden Altar of incense was different from the brazen altar in that on the golden altar no sacrifice was made. The golden altar was the sixth article of furniture in the tabernacle. However, the direction for its construction does not follow the others in chronological order. Between the brazen altar and the altar of incense, God gave Moses instructions concerning the priesthood. There was no need for the altar until there were priests to use it. The golden altar stood as a reminder of the finished work of the brazen altar and the blood that had been shed there.

In Exodus 30:1, 3; God told Moses to make an altar to burn incense upon. This altar was made with Acacia wood (representing the humanity of Christ) and overlaid with gold (representing the deity or divine nature of God). As the two materials of the altar could be distinguished but not divided, so the two-fold nature of Christ as God and man can be seen but not separated. The golden altar shows the work of Christ as priest after His death.

Incense is the symbol of prayer. Psalms 141:2; Let my prayer be set forth before thee as incense. Prayer is in reality what incense was in the symbol. Christ alone is the basis of prayer. The incense for burning on the altar was a special blend given by God, made of four spices. They are:

a.) Stacte - (nataf)

- Stacte was a symbol of the blood of Jesus that was shed on Calvary. It was gathered by making small cuts in the bark to make it bleed out.

b.) Onycha - (shekheleth)

- This spice was a symbol of God's saving power. The original Hebrew word used for this component of the ketoret plant was shecheleth which means to "roar, as a lion; of "peeling off by concussion of sound.". There is confusion of whether it is animal or plant. It is a great medicinal ingredient to bring healing to the whole body. It represented the healing power of prayer.

c.) Galbanum - (Khelbanah)

- This was symbolic of Christ's power not only to save from sin, but also to heal from sin. Galbanum was known for its healing power. Incising the roots of the Ferula plant and collecting the resin obtained it.

d.) Frankincense - (levonah zach)

- It was a symbol of the power of Christ to quicken or revive a man dead in his sins. It was obtained by cutting strips of bark and waiting for three months for the resin to ooze out and harden.

The Golden altar of Incense was constructed with a:

a.) Crown

- The crown of the altar speaks of the exalted Christ, and the success of His intercession for His own.

b.) Horns

- The horns of the altar speak of the power of Christ's intercession, and the power that comes from Him as a result of prayer.

c.) Rings

- The rings speak of the eternal God, who is always present with his people, and who is ready to hear their prayers. It speaks of the power of prayer.

d.) Staves

- The staves speak of Christ as God and man. He brings God and man together at the place of prayer.

The altar of incense was a place of intercession. The prayers of the saints come up as a sweet smelling savor before God. The incense was a symbol of prayers and intercession of the people going up as a sweet smelling fragrance. God wanted His dwelling to be a place where people could approach Him and pray to Him.

Another angel, who had a golden censor, came and stood at the altar. He was given much incense to offer, with the prayers of the saints, on the golden altar before the throne. The smoke of the incense, together with the prayers of the saints went up before God from the angel's hand." (Revelation 8:3-4)

Mercy Seat

Jesus is sitting on the right hand of the Father (God) making intercession for the saints of God. Before His crucifixion and resurrection the Mercy Seat behind the veil was unoccupied. Cherubim were there on both sides of the mercy seat. When Jesus went back and offered up Himself as a sacrifice in heaven for sin, and the offering was received, He now took His place on the Mercy Seat. At the death of Jesus the veil in the temple was rent from top to bottom (Matthew 27:51) removing the curtain that separated God and man. This made it possible for man to make intercession before God, Jesus became the High Priest. Now man can go before God in prayer. Men should always pray and not faint. (Luke 18:1)

The typology of the Old Testament Tabernacle was a glimpse of what was to come through Jesus Christ.

Section 2 Memory Quiz

Scripture to Remember

Exodus 30:1 "And thou shalt make an altar to burn incense upon: of shittim wood shalt thou make it.

Memory Questions

1. The way to the _Golden_ _Altar_ is through the sacrifice at the Brazen Altar.

2. The Golden Altar of Incense was different from the _brazen Altar_ in that on the Golden Altar no _Sacrifice_ is made.

3. _Incense_ is the symbol of prayer.

4. The Golden Altar of Incense was a place of _Prayer_.

5. The typology of the Old Testament Tabernacle was a _Glimpse_ of what was to come through Jesus Christ.

Section 2 Prayer Journal

During and after prayer it is good to write down the thoughts that: come to your mind, people that rise up in your spirit or anything that God will reveal. Learn to write down what God is saying so that you can go back and meditate on what he has revealed to you.

Section 3

Prayer and its Components

I. **What is Prayer?**

Prayer is communication with God. It is an address or petition to God in word or thought; and earnest request or obtained by entreaty. The word prayer, conveys such ideas as ask, request, petition, entreat, supplicate, plead, beseech, beg, implore favor, seek and to enquire.

II. **Dynamics of Prayer**

A. Devotion

B. Trust

C. Respect

D. A sense of dependence on the one to whom we pray

E. Faith

F. Worship

G. Confession

H. Adoration

I. Praise

J. Thanksgiving

K. Dedicated Actions

L. Request

M. Effectiveness

III. Parts of prayer

A. Adoration – Daniel 4:34-35

B. Confession – I John 1:9

C. Supplication – Luke 11:9

D. Intercession – James 5:14-15

E. Thanksgiving – Philippians 4:6

IV. Prayer posture

A. Standing – Nehemiah 9:5

B. Kneeling – Ezra 9:5; Daniel 6:10

C. Sitting – I Chronicles 17:16-27

D. Bowing – Exodus 34:8

E. Hands uplifted – I Timothy 2:8

V. Prayer Times

A. Morning – Psalms 5:3; Mark 1:35

B. Evening – Psalms 4:8; Psalms 141:2; Acts 3:1

C. Three times daily – Psalms 55:17; Daniel 6:10

VI. Prayer Formula – Many times people especially new converts have a hard time knowing how to pray. Here is one formula to follow that will give direction using the acronym ACTS.

A. **A = Adoration** (*The act of adoring; to worship or honor as a deity or divine; to regard with loving adoration and devotion*).

B. **C = Confession** (*A disclosure of one's sins in the sacrament of reconciliation; to acknowledge your sins to God*).

C. **T = Thanksgiving** (*A prayer confessing gratitude; the act of giving thanks.*

D. **S = Supplication** (*To pray to God; asking for earnestly and humbly*).

VII. Hindrances to prayer

A. Psalms 66:18
If I regard iniquity in my heart, the Lord will not hear me.

B. John 9:31
Now we know that God heareth not sinners: but if any man be a worshipper of God, and doeth His will, him He heareth.

C. James 4:3
Ye ask, and receive not, because ye ask amiss, that ye may consume it upon your lusts.

D. Job 27:8
For what is the hope of the hypocrite, though he hath gained, when God taketh away his soul.

E. Job 27:9
Will God hear his cry when trouble cometh upon him?

VIII. Having confidence that He hears

A. I John 5:14-15

14 And this is the confidence that we have in Him, that, if we ask any thing according to his will, he heareth us:

15 And if we know he hear us, whatsoever we ask, we know that we have the petitions that we have of him.

B. I John 3:22

And whatsoever we ask, we receive of him, because we keep his commandments, and do those things that are pleasing in his sight.

C. Isaiah 38:1-8

Hezekiah and his prayer to God to prolong his life

Section 3 Memory Quiz

Scripture to Remember

John 9:31 "Now we know that God heareth not sinners: but if any man be a worshipper of God, and doeth His will, him He heareth.

Memory Questions

1. The word "prayer" conveys such ideas as _earnest_, request, entreat, _supplicate_, plead, beg, _implore_, favor, seek and to inquire.

2. Prayer postures are standing, _kneeling_, sitting, _Bowing_ and hands uplifted.

3. _____ is an acronym of prayer.

4. If I regard _iniquity_ in my heart, the Lord will not _hear_ me.

5. _Thanksgiving_ is a prayer confessing gratitude, the act of giving thanks.

Section 3 Prayer Journal

During and after prayer it is good to write down the thoughts that: come to your mind, people that rise up in your spirit or anything that God will reveal. Learn to write down what God is saying so that you can go back and meditate on what he has revealed to you.

Section 4

Prayer Watch: Praying for at least 1 hour

I. In Matthew 26:40:

Jesus prayed three times in the Garden of Gethsemane, after the first time He found Peter, James and John (Matthew 26:40) asleep, and He asked them ... "could you not watch with me for one hour?"

You should at least pray constantly for one hour, but if you do not have a plan, you will get weary and give up. A plan for praying at least one hour is divided into twelve (12) five minute segments as follows:

1. Praise (first 5 minutes) complimenting God on what He has done.

2. Pray for people in authority specifically governmental leaders etc. (I Timothy 2:1-4)

3. Thanksgiving (give thanks for everything).

4. Binding the power of Satan (bind distractions, sleeping spirits, drowsiness, slumber, fatigue, anger or any other spirits that the Holy Spirit reveals to you).

5. Pray for the lost (make a list of those that are lost and pray for them continuously).

6. Loose the angels of the Lord (God has assigned angels to the saints and we can petition God to send them to aid us in the battle).

7. Pray for "the body of Christ" (your local church and other churches and pray for your pastor and other pastors).

8. Pray for the Holy Spirit to be in control.

9. Pray for your family specifically for (the lost, illnesses, those that are battling forces).

10. Pray for God to raise up a standard in (Congress, the Senate, Supreme Court, School systems, Family etc.).

11. Pray for the needs of others (make a list of all those that you told you would pray for them so that you fulfill your word).

12. Praise (begins with praise and end with praise).

II. After you've prayed wait on God, give Him the opportunity to speak. Know that when you pray and peace follows that you've prayer through effectively. God will always lead you by peace. Jesus said; *Peace I leave with you, My peace I give to you; not as the world gives do I give to you. (John 14:27a)*

Another Acronym for Prayer:

P = Position

R = Reverence

A = Attitude

Y = Yielding (God's will be done)

E = Effort

R = Rest (Faith)

Section 4 Memory Quiz

Scripture to Remember

Matthew 26:40 "And he cometh unto the disciples, and findeth them asleep, and saith unto Peter, 'What, could ye not watch with me for one hour?'

Memory Questions

1. Peter, James and John went to the *Garden* of *Gethsemane* with Jesus.

2. After you've prayed *wait* on God, give Him the *opportunity* to speak.

3. God will always lead by *peace* .

4. Pray for the *Holy Spirit* _____ to be in control.

5. Acronyms: P= position; *Reverence* A= attitude; *yielding* E= effort; R= rest.

Section 4 Prayer Journal

During and after prayer it is good to write down the thoughts that: come to your mind, people that rise up in your spirit or anything that God will reveal. Learn to write down what God is saying so that you can go back and meditate on what he has revealed to you.

Section 5

God Answers Prayer

When you pray to God you must have the faith to believe that He hears, and when He (God) hears He will cause it to come to fruition. Pray believing. Search out scriptures that agree with what you are praying about. When you pray, pray the will of God, which is His Word. Use scripture references to solidify your prayers. Use scriptures like:

I John 5:14 And this is the confidence that we have in him, that if we ask anything according to his will he heareth us:

15 And if we know that he hears us, whatsoever we ask, we know that we have the petitions that we desired of him.

II Chronicles 7:14 If my people, which are called by my name, shall humble themselves, and pray, and seek my face, and turn from their wicked ways, then will I hear from heaven, and will forgive their sin, and will heal their land.

15 Now mine eyes shall be open, and mine ears attent unto the prayer that is made in this place.

16 For now have I chosen and sanctified this house, that my name may be there forever: and mine eyes and mine heart shall be there perpetually.

Praying the "Word of God" helps us that we pray not amiss to our own lusts. James 4:3 (NIV) "When you ask, you do not receive, because you ask with wrong motives, that you may spend what you get on your own pleasures." When you go to God asking, ask in faith and trusting Him with all your heart.

David was a man after God's own heart and he prayed to God earnestly and God blessed him and answered according to his petition. David had been to battle and came back to Ziklag, but when he came back he found that the Amalekites had burned their city and took their families captive. David's two wives Ahinoam and Abigail were taken also. His men were so distraught they thought of stoning David. But David, leader and King, even though he cried and his heart was heavy had "to encourage himself, in the Lord."

He asked Abiathar the Priest to bring the ephod and David prayed to God for the answer. He knew he needed help to retrieve his family and belongings. David asked God shall I pursue after them? God's answer to David was to "Pursue; for thou shalt surely overtake them, and without fail recover all." David and the men of Judah went to battle and David recovered all that the Amalekites had taken including their wives, children, cattle and even the spoil.

An example of another person was Daniel. For twenty-one (21) days Daniel set his face to seek the Lord. He prayed, fasted, made confessions and interceded not only for himself but for the people. In the book of Daniel he spoke to God saying:

> *Daniel 9:5 "We have sinned, and have committed iniquity, and have done wickedly, and have rebelled, even by departing from thy precepts and from thy judgments:*
>
> *6 Neither have we hearkened unto thy servants the prophets, which spake in thy name...*

Daniel was persistent and while he was still speaking and confessing and presenting his supplications God sent Gabriel. Gabriel said, "At the beginning of the supplication the commandment came forth and I am come to shew thee; (Daniel 9:23). But before I could get you the answer the prince of Persia withstood me one and twenty days, so Michael came and helped me. Daniels' prayer was heard and answered the very first day that he prayed. Whatever it takes God will answer for He said to Jeremiah in (Jeremiah 33:3)

> *"Call unto me, and I will answer thee, and shew thee great and mighty things, which thou knowest not."*

The answer was not only for that time but for times to come. Pray and keep on praying until you see your petitions come to fruition.

Another example is Jehosphat, Jehosaphat received word that the Ammonites, the Moabites and a great multitude of forces had aligned themselves against him and the children of Judah. Jehosphat realized that these forces were mightier and greater that what was with him and if they didn't get help they would be defeated. So he set his face to seek the Lord and gathered all of the people of Judah so that they could "ask help of the Lord." Without a doubt he had to trust God to send help from on high; ... God is a very present help in the time of trouble

(Ps. 46:1). As they fasted and prayed God spoke through Jahaziel to the people. He told them "Be not dismayed by reason of this great multitude; for the battle is not yours' but God's. The prophet gave Jehosphat instructions from God and as he followed the instructions given by the prophet; God won the battle. God caused the enemy to fight against themselves, not one of them escaped. God said for Jehosphat and the children of Judah to "believe in the Lord thy God so shall ye be established; believe His prophets so shall ye prosper." Jeshosphat saw his enemies destroyed and walked away with the spoils. He put his trust in God and sought him for the answer.

God did not disappoint them he fought the battle for them. Prayer changes things.

God answers prayer, trust in Him. Don't put your confidence in material things or things that are temporal. Temporal things are temporary not eternal. Set your affections on things above and not on things of the earth.

Don't focus on getting the answer in a specific way. Trust God to send it in whatever way He wants to send it. However God works it out be open for He knows what is best for you. Wait on the Lord and be of good courage and he shall strengthen thine heart, wait, I say, on the Lord (Psalms 27:14).

Section 5 Memory Quiz

Scripture to Remember

II Chronicles 7:14 "If My people, which are called by my name, shall humble themselves, and pray, and seek my face, and turn from their wicked ways, then will I hear from heaven, and will forgive their sin, and will heal their land.

Memory Questions

1. Praying the _Word_ of _God_ helps us that we pray not amiss to our own lusts.

2. God's answer to David was to "_Pursue_; for thou shall surely _overtake_ them and without fail recover all."

3. Pray and keep on praying until you see your petitions come to _fruition_.

4. _Prayer_ changes things.

5. Wait on the Lord, and be of good courage and he shall _strengthen_ thine heart.

Section 5 Prayer Journal

During and after prayer it is good to write down the thoughts that come to your mind, people that rise up in your spirit or anything that God will reveal. Learn to write down what God is saying so that you can go back and meditate on what he has revealed to you.

Section 6

Prayer Triggers

The Lord often communicates his burden to intercede through triggers. A "trigger" is defined as a lever pressed by the fingers to discharge a firearm; or any similar devices used to stimulate a mechanism; a stimulus.

"Prayer triggers" signal or alerts you that it is time to pray. Even though we are to always pray and not faint and to pray without ceasing the Holy Spirit will give you an unction to pray. It is important to know by what means the Holy Spirit prompts you when it's time to pray and intercede. "Knowledge is power," to know how to recognize these triggers will help you to understand and discern when to pray.

1. Heaviness in your mind - You know that you are not in sin, the family is fine, and yet that heaviness remains over you. This is the Lord's way of saying "Go Pray." (Matthew 11:28-30)

2. Overwhelming desire to weep – This comes suddenly and for no known reason. (Romans 8:26)

3. A mental picture of something or someone that flashes into your mind. (Acts 21:10-11)

4. An intense longing to be alone with God. (Psalms 42:1-2)

5. A dream or vision. (Acts 2:17-18)

6. A physical weakness such as Daniel's experience. (Daniel 8:17-18; 27)

7. A dull heart ache. (Romans 9:2)

8. A burning in the pit of the stomach. (Luke 24:32)

9. A sense of feeling flushed. (Isaiah 40:29-31)

10. A small quiet voice in your mind saying to pray. (Matthew 14:23, Luke 6:12)

11. A sense of emergency. (Daniel 7:13)

12. A flash of a name or face across your mind. (Acts 9:10-14)

Section 6 Memory Quiz

Memory Questions

1. What is a Prayer Trigger? _____
   _____
   _____

2. _____ is power.

3. Prayer triggers _____
   or alerts you that it's time to pray.

4. Who prompts you to pray and alerts you when
   things are urgent needs? _____
   _____

5. _____ _____ is the Lord's.

Section 6 Prayer Journal

During and after prayer it is good to write down the thoughts that: come to your mind, people that rise up in your spirit or anything that God will reveal. Learn to write down what God is saying so that you can go back and meditate on what he has revealed to you.

Section 7

Intercession

I. What is intercession?

Intercession is the act of petitioning God on behalf of another person or group. The Greek noun, "enteuxus" denotes a "meeting with," a conversation or petition rendered on behalf of another. Seeking the presence and audience of God in another's stead. The scripture reference comes from Ezekiel 22:30; I looked for a man among them who would build up the wall and stand before me in the gap on behalf of the land so I would not have to destroy it, but I found none. In times of war, when the enemy's assault left gaps in the city walls, leaders defended their cities by standing in the broken areas of the wall to protect the people.

II. Relationship – You will pass through four stages:

A. Acquaintance – Through the new birth you become acquainted with God as His child.

B. Friendship – Beyond getting acquainted with God you develop a true friendship with Him.

C. Trust – This is based on your friendship and the experiences you've had with Him. As this is initiated then trust is activated.

D. Intimacy – Trust is the doorway to intimacy.

III. Burden and Responsibility – True intercession bears a burden and responsibility.

A. Prayer - Ezra 10:1; Nehemiah 1:4; Isaiah 22:4; Jeremiah 13:17; Jeremiah 23:9

B. Fasting – Deuteronomy 9:8-9; Deuteronomy 9:12-20; Ezra 10:6

IV. Intercessors nature

A. Persistent and determined – Isaiah 62:6-7; Lamentations 2:18-19

B. Humility – Colossians 3:12; I Peter 5:5; James 4:6

C. Compassion – Jude 22; Lamentations 3:22-23

D. Integrity

E. Servant hood

F. Purity

G. Intimacy

H. Faith

I. Selflessness

J. Self-Discipline

V. Intercessory Prayer should be focused continually on:

A. Leaders and government authorities – I Timothy 2:12

B. People of God – Joel 2:2-13; Romans 1:9; Ephesians 6:18

C. Pastors and Leaders – II Corinthians 1:11; I Thessalonians 5:25; Hebrews 13:17-18

D. Communities – Psalms 112:6; Jeremiah 29:7; Daniel 9:3

Section 7 Memory Quiz

Scripture to Remember

Ezekiel 22:30 "I looked for a man among them who would build up the wall and stand before me in the gap on behalf of the land so I would not have to destroy it, but I found none.

Memory Questions

1. _____ is the act of petitioning God on behalf of another person or group.

2. True intercession bears a _____ and responsibility.

3. _____ is the doorway to intimacy.

4. "I exhort therefore, that first of all, supplications, _____ intercessions, and giving of _____, be made for all men;" (I Timothy 2:1)

5. Beyond getting _____ with God you develop a _____ with Him.

Section 7 Prayer Journal

During and after prayer it is good to write down the thoughts that: come to your mind, people that rise up in your spirit or anything that God will reveal. Learn to write down what God is saying so that you can go back and meditate on what he has revealed to you.

Section 8

Worship the Lord in Spirit and in Truth

I. What is worship?

The word worship comes from the Greek word "prokuneo" which means to fall down or bow down before a deity. Worship has nothing to do with your physical posture; it is a place of reverencing God. True worship comes out of your relationship with God. We bow down to the true and living God.

II. What kind of worship does God require?

1. True Worship

A. True worship is an expression of true praise. This level of worship comes from knowing the God who loves you and gave His life for you. This level of worship comes out an authentic relationship with Him. We worship him (God) from our inner most being. An example of a true worshipper was David. David was a man after God's own heart whose life was a life of worship. When David was told that the Ark of the Covenant which represented the presence of God, was in Obededom's house and everything that he possessed was blessed because of the Ark being in his house. David went to retrieve the Ark and bring it back to the city of David. The Ark of the Covenant was behind the veil in the tabernacle prototype and could only be approached once a year by the High Priest. David knew the importance of having "the Spirit of God" (Ark) with his people.

The "Ark of the Covenant" was a box or chest that contained the golden pot of manna, Aaron's rod that budded, and the Laws (Ten Commandments). It was covered with a top which was called the "Mercy Seat." The Mercy Seat was placed on top of the Ark and had two cherubim on each side of the seat to protect it. This was a prototype of what was to come. When Jesus would sacrifice His life and offer up His blood for the sins of His people and then occupy His place on the Mercy Seat. At this point, the cherubim would no longer have to protect the place where only Jesus could occupy. He (Jesus) is on the right hand of the Father (God) crying mercy for the saints of God.

David knew its importance and as he was bringing it back (II Samuel 6:13-15) he worshipped God by stopping after six paces and offering oxen and fatlings as a sacrifice unto God. David danced with all his might before the

Ark. As the Ark came back into the city of David he leaped and danced and offered burnt offerings and peace offerings before the Lord. He was not concerned about his position as King; he adored the King of Kings and Lord of Lords. When his wife critized him for the way he acted before the people, David was not ashamed. He told his wife Michal according to (II Samuel 6:20-22);

20 Then David returned to bless his household. And his wife Michal daughter of Saul came out to meet David and said, How glorious was the King of Israel today, who stripped himself of his kingly robes and uncovered himself in the eyes of his servant maids as one of the worthless fellows shamelessly uncovers himself!

21 David said to Michal, It was before the Lord, who chose me above your Father and all his house to appoint me as prince of Israel, the people of the Lord. Therefore will I make merry (in pure enjoyment) of the Lord.

22 I will be still more lightly esteemed than this, and will humble and lower myself in my own sight (and yours). But by the maids you mentioned, I will be held in honor.

David was not ashamed to worship the one and only true God. The God that said I am a jealous

God and will have you to worship no other God before me.

2. In Spirit and in Truth

Jesus speaking to the Samaritan woman (John 4:22) said:

22 "Ye worship you know not what; we know what we worship, for salvation is of the Jews." **He goes on to say in** *(John 4:23-24);*

23 But the hour cometh, and now is, when the true worshippers shall worship the Father in spirit and in truth: for the Father seeketh such to worship Him:

24 God is a spirit and they that worship Him must worship Him in spirit and in truth."

III. True Worship versus False Worship

Another example is Nebuchadnezzar, the king of Babylon, which required the people of Babylon to bow down and worship him. If that was not enough he built a statue of himself and required everyone to bow down and worship his image. This statue represented him as their god. Shadrach, Meshach, and Abednego were brought to Babylon as exiles from Israel and worshipped the Lord God Almighty, Jehovah God, the I Am the only true God. They refused to bow down to the statue because their laws require that they shall have no other God but Jehovah God or bow down to any but Him. God admonished them through the laws not to make any image (Exodus 20:4);

Thou shall not make unto thee any graven image, or any likeness of anything that is in the heaven above, or that is in the earth beneath, or that is in the water under the earth:

The three Hebrew boys would not bow down to the image but was willing to endure the consequences because of their love and devotion to God. If you love me you will keep my commandments (I John 2:3). The Hebrew boys knew that their God could deliver them. If He chose not to it was not because he couldn't. They were told as they heard the sound of the cymbals and the other instruments that initiated worship to the image, that they should fall down and worship and if they didn't they would be thrown into the fiery furnace. They chose not to worship the idol so they were thrown into the furnace. When the king came back expecting to see ashes and bones he saw four men walking around in the fire; the fourth looking like the "Son of Man." Then Nebuchadnezzar commanded the Babylonian people to worship the God of Shadrach, Meshach and Abednego. He also advanced them in the kingdom. Worship God and Him alone, for He is worthy to receive glory, and honor and praises.

Section 8 Memory Quiz

Scripture to Remember

John 4:24 "God is a Spirit: and they that worship him must worship him in spirit and in truth.

Memory Questions

1. _____ has nothing to do with your _____ posture.

2. David was not _____ to _____ the one and only true God.

3. The "Ark of the Covenant" was a box that contained the golden pot of manna, _____ that _____, and the _____.

4. Worship is a place to _____ down or _____ down to a deity.

5. The three Hebrew boys would not bow down to the image; but was willing to endure the consequences because of _____ _____ and _____ to God.

Section 8 Prayer Journal

During and after prayer it is good to write down the thoughts that: come to your mind, people that rise up in your spirit or anything that God will reveal. Learn to write down what God is saying so that you can go back and meditate on what he has revealed to you.

Section 9

Prayer Points

a. Prayer for Salvation

b. Prayer for the infilling of the Holy Spirit

c. Prayer for Healing

d. Prayer for Deliverance

e. Prayer for Financial Breakthrough

Prayer for Salvation

Scriptures:

John 3:16

> For God so loved the world that he gave his only begotten Son, that whosoever believeth in Him should not perish, but have everlasting life.

Romans 10:9

> That if thou shall confess with thy mouth the Lord Jesus, and shalt believe in thine heart that God hath raised him from the dead, thou shalt be saved.

Acts 2:21

> And it shall come to pass, that whosoever shall call on the name of the Lord, shall be saved.

Prayer:

Father God, in the name of Jesus, we thank you for Jesus Christ who shed His blood on Calvary for our sins. For without the shedding of blood there is no remission for sin. We thank you Lord for bridging the gap between You (God) and man that was breached in the Garden of Eden.

Father God, as an act of my will I confess Jesus Christ as my Lord and Saviour, and ask You to forgive me of all sin, transgressions and iniquities that I have committed. Father God, I confess with my mouth the Lord Jesus, and I believe in my heart, that He is the "Son of God;" that He died and was resurrected from the dead. I believe that through his death, burial and resurrection that *I am saved*.

I receive (Jesus Christ) as my Lord and Saviour. I accept salvation through His blood.

Today I decree and declare that I am saved and have entered the family of God through faith in Jesus Christ.

Thank You Lord for Salvation.

Prayer for the Infilling of the Holy Spirit

Scriptures:

John 3:5-6

> 5 Jesus answered, I say unto thee, Except a man be born of water and of the Spirit, he cannot enter into the kingdom of God.
>
> 6 That which is born of the flesh is flesh; and that which is born of the Spirit is spirit.

Romans 8:11

> But if the Spirit of him that raised up Jesus from the dead dwell in you, he that raised up Christ from the dead shall also quicken your mortal bodies by his Spirit that dwells in you.

Acts 2:4

> And they were all filled with the Holy Ghost, and began to speak with tongues, as the Spirit gave them utterance.

Acts 8:15-17

> 15 Who, when they were come down prayed for them, that they might receive the Holy Ghost:
>
> 16 (For as yet he was fallen upon none of them: only they were baptized in the name of the Lord Jesus)
>
> 17 Then laid they their hands on them; and they received the Holy Ghost.

Prayers:

Father God, in the name of Jesus. I thank You that You did not leave us comfortless but You sent us back of Your Holy Spirit to not only dwell with us but live in us. Thank You that through faith in the name of Jesus we received salvation.

Now Father, according to your word you said to ask and it shall be given. I now ask You to fill me with Your Holy Spirit. Let the Holy Ghost dwell richly within me to empower me to live a saved and disciplined life before you.

Let Him comfort me, lead me, reveal to me and teach me all things. Let the fruit of the Holy Spirit began to manifest in my life. Let love abound more and more. Let the works of the flesh be destroyed that I might produce fruit worthy of repentance. Let the Holy Spirit manifest itself with the evidence of speaking with other tongues.

Father God, give me the temperance to move out of the way and let the Holy Spirit lead me and guide me in the way of holiness. Let every footstep that I take be ordered and directed by the Holy Ghost.

Father God, I thank You for answering my prayers and infilling me with Your Holy Spirit. Let the fruit of the Holy Spirit according to Galatians 5:22-23 become visible in my life.

I receive it by faith in Jesus name.

Prayer for Healing

Scriptures:

Psalms 107:20

> He sent his word, and healed them, and delivered them from their destructions.

Isaiah 53:5

> But he was wounded for our transgressions, he was bruised for our iniquities: the chastisement of our peace was upon him; and with his stripes we are healed.

James 5:14-15

> 14 Is any sick among you? Let him call for the elders of the church; and let them pray over him, anointing him with oil in the name of the Lord:

> 15 And the prayer of faith shall save the sick, and the Lord shall raise him up, and if he have committed sins, they shall be forgiven him.

Prayer

Father God, in the name of Jesus, we call upon the matchless name of Jesus Christ. You said to call and you would answer, and show us great and mighty things that we know not of (Jeremiah 33:3).

Today we ask that you would heal all that are sick. We are believing you to deliver, heal and make whole all that are sick from inherited diseases; diabetes, cancer, high blood pressure, and any thing that would be passed down through the generational bloodline. Father God, I ask that You heal from every infirmity, all viral infections, all bacterial infections, any thing that will cause your people problems in their bodies.

Father, you said You wished above all things that we would prosper and be in health, even as our soul doth prosper. Lord, thank You for sending your word and healing us from all of our destructions. Father, we thank you for directing us to the elders whom You have anointed to lay hands on the sick we pray that they will rise up and make themselves available (James 5:13-15)

Father God, thank You that by the stripes of Jesus we are healed

We stand firm on the Word of God and accept our healing. We stand on faith believing that every sickness, every disease, every infirmity, is healed by the power of God. I decree that no weapon formed against us (no sickness, disease or infirmity) is going to proper. In the matchless name of Jesus it is so. We claim it in Jesus name.

Prayer for Deliverance

Scriptures:

II Timothy 3:10-11

> 10 But thou has fully known my doctrine, manner of life, purpose, faith, longsuffering, charity, patience,

> 11 Persecutions, afflictions, which came unto me at Antioch, at Iconium, at Lystra; what persecutions I endured; but out of them all the Lord delivered me.

II Timothy 4:18

> And the Lord shall deliver me from every evil work, and will preserve me unto his heavenly kingdom: to whom be glory for ever and ever. Amen.

II Peter 2:9

> The Lord knoweth how to deliver the godly out of temptation: and to reserve the unjust unto the day of judgement to be punished.

Psalms 34:17

> The righteous cry, and the Lord heareth, and delivereth them out of all their troubles.

Isaiah 59:1

> Behold, the Lord's hand is not shortened, that it cannot save; neither his ear heavy, that it cannot hear;

Prayer:

Father God, in the name of Jesus. I know that you will deliver. The word of God says that the thief comes to steal, kill and destroy but you come to give life and that more abundantly. I thank you for delivering my mind, from evil thoughts, for helping me to guard my heart and helping me to walk in the straight and narrow path.

Father, I praise you for your delivering power, delivering from generational curses, generational diseases, and generational poverty. Deliver me from anything that would cause havoc in my life. Today in my generation it stops, right here, right now.

Father God, I receive deliverance from any hatred, anger, bitterness or wrath that I might be harboring against anyone. I choose as an act of my will to forgive any and every person that have hurt me or harmed me. I choose to let them go, that I go free. I receive healing from hurts, wounds that will cause evil roots to manifest in my life. Lord, deliver and destroy every evil root. Deliver me from the roots of rejection, persecution, offenses, anxieties, depression, oppression or anything that would contaminate my life. Your Word says that You would deliver me out of all my troubles. I receive that deliverance. I stand on your word; I am delivered and set free. In Jesus name.

Prayer for Financial Breakthrough

Scriptures:

Matthew 6:33-34

> 33 But seek ye first the kingdom of God, and his righteousness; and all these things shall be added unto you.

> 34 Take therefore no thought for the morrow: for the morrow shall take thought for the things of itself. Sufficient unto the day is the evil thereof:

II Chronicles 20:20

> ... Believe in the Lord your God, so shall ye be established; believe his prophets, so shall ye prosper.

Luke 6:38

> Give, and it shall be given unto you; good measure, pressed down, and shaken together, and running over, shall men give into your bosom. For with the same measure that ye mete withal is shall be measured to you again.

Matthew 13:12

> For whosoever hath, to him shall be given, and he shall have more abundance: but whosoever hath not, from him shall be taken away even that he hath.

3 John 2

> Beloved, I wish above all things that thou mayest prosper and be in health, even as thy soul prosper.

Prayer

Father God, in the name of Jesus. I call upon Your Holy name and give You thanks and glory for all that you do for us. Thank You for financial breakthrough. Thank you for helping us to follow the plan that is written in Your word. You told us to give and it shall be given. We freely give to the kingdom of God.

Thank you for blessing us richly with the finances so that we can freely give to the kingdom. Help us to be faithful tithe payers, and give offerings that are well pleasing to you. Help us to seek you first, and according to your word everything else will be added unto us.

Father, I pray that we will not be slaves to debt. We thank you for financial freedom. I decree and declare that every debt is destroyed through the blood of Jesus. I thank you that I am debt free.

Lord, speak to our hearts that we will give the way you desire for us to give. Help us not to hold back but give freely and cheerfully. You said for every man to give according to the way he purposed in his heart; not grudgingly, or of necessity: for God loveth a cheerful giver. Father, we thank you that it is you (God) that gives us the power to get wealth.

Jesus You became a curse for us when You hung on a tree. Lord, we receive deliverance from every spirit of generational poverty. Give this generation a different mind to know that it is your will for your people to be blessed. Help us not to hold on to words that discourage. Help us to depend on you. Help us not to have a love for money but to be balanced in our attitude toward giving and receiving from God.

Lord, we choose to worship you and not mammon. Deliver us from greed, love of money, or anything that will make money more important than you (God). Help us to balance our desire to work with our love for God and trust God to take care of all of our needs.

WE give bountifully according to your word that says that "he which soweth sparingly shall reap also sparingly; and he which soweth bountifully shall reap also bountifully.

Thank you God, for financial breakthrough in our giving and receiving from You. Everything that we have belongs to you. Thank you that we will obey you even in our giving. We bless you for it now in Jesus name.

References

1. The American Heritage Dictionary of the English Language William Morris, Editor

2. Dictionary.com

3. New Open Bible – King James Version Thomas Nelson Publishers

4. Articles and Papers by Dr. Curtis D. Ward (Mending broken Lives, and Setting the Captive Free) Posted March4, 2010

CPSIA information can be obtained at www.ICGtesting.com
Printed in the USA
LVOW07s1254280913

354498LV00007B/114/P